S Y D N E

Sydney is the largest city in Australia with a population of over four million people. From its beginnings as the first European settlement in eastern Australia, Sydney has grown to become one of the most vibrant cities in the world. Tall buildings dominate the central business district (CBD), but it is the remarkable harbour, with its many bays, coves, inlets and rivers that captures the visitor's attention.

While the CBD is the commercial centre, there are many other focal points. Darling Harbour offers wonderful dining, shopping and recreation, while Oxford Street and Kings Cross offer great food and coffee in a more Bohemian setting. Chinatown is renowned for its restaurants specialising in regional Chinese cuisine. The Rocks gives a glimpse of Sydney's early history, while the Royal Botanic Gardens and the neighbouring park, the Domain, provide fresh, green spaces in the city's heart.

What is exceptional about Sydney is its diversity, embodied in its harmonious, multicultural community. This diversity is reflected in the amazing range of food available – from European to village Asian to spicy Middle Eastern and African, and a developing, distinctively Australian cuisine.

The waters of the Harbour and the Tasman Sea are the outstanding features of Sydney. On the Harbour, the ferries and pleasure craft provide transport and recreation. The beaches with their surf and sand are made for relaxing.

All these ingredients together make up the Sydney of today.

Above: *The gun's gone and competing yachts are beating into a stiff nor'easter!* **Opposite:** *A view of Sydney Harbour from above Rose Bay, Double Bay, Rushcutters Bay, Woolloomooloo Bay and Farm Cove draws the eye toward the city, bordered by the Royal Botanic Gardens and the Domain.* **Following pages:** *A view of the CBD and adjoining areas from North Sydney.*

A MARVELLOUS HARBOUR

Sydney is situated on the beautiful harbour known as Port Jackson. Captain James Cook, the English navigator who explored and mapped the east coast of Australia in 1770, noted this harbour but did not enter it. In 1788, Governor Arthur Phillip arrived with the First Fleet to establish the first European settlement. He liked what he saw of Port Jackson: a magnificent harbour that offered a haven for ships, a water supply at the head of a cove that he named Sydney Cove, and a situation where an isolated settlement would be safe from bombardment from the sea.

The sandstone headlands that define the harbour are the visible remains of a drowned river valley. Unlike many estuaries, Sydney Harbour has its highest sandstone cliffs on the coast.

Sydney has always been a port. Its deep water provides excellent berthing for the world's largest ocean liners and for cargo and container ships plying their commercial trade.

Top: *North Head and South Head with the Sydney CBD in the background.* **Middle:** *Lady Martins Beach, Felix Bay, Point Piper.*
Bottom: *Looking across the cliffs of The Gap to Watsons Bay and down the Harbour to the city.*

Above: *Looking north east towards the Heads with Woolloomooloo Bay, Potts Point and Kings Cross in the foreground. Beyond are Rushcutters Bay and the yachts of the Cruising Yacht Club of Australia. Clarke and Shark Islands stand guard.* **Below:** *(Left) Camp Cove and Green Point with Watsons Bay behind, in a view looking south towards Bondi. (Right) Doyle's famous fish restaurant right on the beach at Watsons Bay.*

Above: *Pedestrians and the monorail use the old Pyrmont Bridge to cross Darling Harbour. The AMP Tower at Centrepoint overlooks it all.*
Below: *(Left) Ponds and running water are features of the Darling Harbour complex. (Right) Cockle Bay Wharf and marina.*

DARLING HARBOUR

Darling Harbour was originally called Cockle Bay. Here the Wangal clan of the Iora Aboriginal people used to gather shellfish.

The Darling Harbour complex is on the site of a former railway goods yard. An imaginative plan sought to convert this area into the shopping and recreational complex we see today. The complex was opened in 1988, 200 years after the arrival of the First Fleet.

Darling Harbour is within easy walking distance of the city. It can also be reached by monorail or by ferry from Circular Quay. A tram from Central Railway Station also passes close to Darling Harbour.

Top: *The Darling Harbour complex and adjacent hotels viewed from the old Pyrmont Bridge.*
Above: *The South Steyne, a retired Manly ferry, and the Bounty replica moored on the western side of Darling Harbour.*

Top: *The Sydney Aquarium with walk-through viewing of its collection of marine life.*
Above: *Cruise and charter boats moored near the Sydney Aquarium.*

Top: (Left) The Australian Maritime Museum with its collection of historic boats and ships moored alongside. (Right) A gallery interior in the Australian Maritime Museum.
Centre: (Left) The shell-like exterior of the Australian Maritime Museum. (Right) A sculpture symbolically connecting Aboriginal history and culture with Darling Harbour.
Below: (Left) The pagoda, a focus of the Chinese Gardens, was a gift from the people of China for Australia's bicentenary. (Right) The entrance to the Chinese Gardens.

Above: *The Sydney Harbour Bridge spans the harbour from Dawes Point near the CBD to Milsons Point, from where this photo was taken, on the north shore. At night, the bridge is illuminated with a pale incandescent light.* **Below:** *The lights of the CBD from the north shore.*

Above: *A luxury liner berthed at the Overseas Passenger Terminal at Circular Quay. The ships add to the fiesta of lights that surround the Quay, complementing the illuminated arch of the Harbour Bridge and the graceful light-bathed roof of the Opera House.*

HARBOUR LIGHTS

As evening descends, a myriad lights in a rainbow of colours slowly spread over the Harbour, to be reflected in the busy waters. Thousands of lights illuminate the skyscrapers of the CBD, and the span and pylons of the Sydney Harbour Bridge.

After the sun goes down, the night-life begins. The Rocks restaurants welcome their dinner guests. The bars, nightclubs and pubs move into high gear, offering many kinds of music, from Latin to jazz to rock. East Circular Quay lures Opera House pedestrians in for a tasty meal and a drink before the performance.

Above: *The Opera House with the Royal Botanic Gardens in the background.*
Opposite: *The Opera House, with the Harbour Bridge as a backdrop, seen from the western shoreline of Mrs Macquarie's Point. The foreground is dominated by a Port Jackson fig tree. These magnificent trees are common on the foreshores of Sydney Harbour.*

SYDNEY OPERA HOUSE

The Sydney Opera House was designed by the Danish architect Joern Utzon.

A competition was held to find the best design. Two hundred and thirty designs were submitted by architects from 33 countries. Utzon's design discarded conventional walls and roofs, with the auditoriums protected by giant shells intended to rise like sails above the base of the building and the Harbour. Initially the building was to have no apron, so as to give it the appearance of floating on the water. The Sydney Opera House was officially opened by Queen Elizabeth II on 20 October 1973; however, the first paying performance (of the Australian Opera's production of Prokofiev's *War and Peace*) took place on 28 September 1973.

Top: *The shells, closed off with double-glazed, tinted glass, viewed from the forecourt.*
Middle: *The Opera House from Farm Cove.* **Bottom:** *The Opera House as seen from a ferry nearing Circular Quay.*

Above: *Directly above the Opera House with the Concert Theatre (2690 seats), Drama Theatre (544 seats) and Playhouse Theatre (398 seats) on the left-hand side and the Opera Theatre (1547 seats) on the right-hand side. The Bennelong Restaurant is just in view in the foreground.*

Below: *(Left) The interior of the Concert Hall. (Right) Steps leading from the forecourt to the performance areas.*

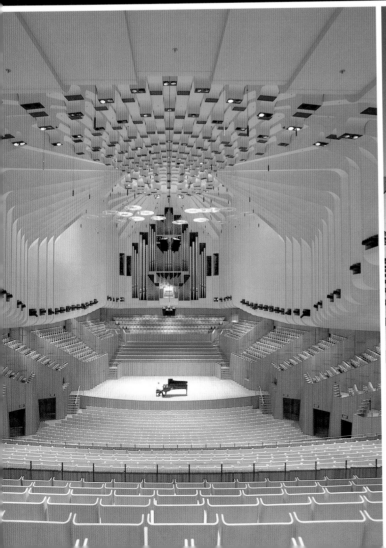

Above: *Looking east to the Opera House on Bennelong Point.*
Opposite: *The Opera House and the Sydney Harbour Bridge at sunset, viewed from Mrs Macquarie's Point, looking west.*

SYDNEY HARBOUR BRIDGE

The Sydney Harbour Bridge was designed by John Bradfield and built by Dorman Long, an English company.

The span is a two-hinged arch bridge with a steel deck hanging from the arch. The arch is hinged at the bottom of each pylon, which allows for movement in the structure, and also takes the weight of the bridge. The pylons are hollow and are largely decorative.

The arch was constructed in two halves. Each half, supported by huge steel cables, is anchored into U-shaped tunnels excavated into the sandstone rock.

The Sydney Harbour Bridge was opened on Saturday, 19 March 1932, by the New South Wales Premier, Jack Lang, but only after officials had re-tied the ceremonial ribbon that had been cut by Captain Francis De Groot, who was a member of the New Guard, a group opposed to Lang.

Above: *The Bridge looking north from the old bond stores at The Rocks: a view much admired by Sydney artist Grace Cossington-Smith.*

Top: *The view towards the CBD from Milsons Point.*
Below: *The Harbour Bridge frames the western sky glowing with the deepening colours of dusk.*

Above: *Walking over the top arch of the Bridge is now very much a part of an adventurous visit to Sydney.*

Below: *The Australian flag and the New South Wales State flag fly over the Bridge and are illuminated at night.*

Top: *(Left) The Anzac Bridge joins Pyrmont to Glebe Island. At the top of the eastern pylon flies the Australian flag, while the New Zealand flag flies atop the western pylon. (Right) The castellated stone facades of the bridge joining Cammeray to Northbridge. The roadway is supported on a concrete arch.* **Above:** *The footbridge at Darling Harbour looking towards the Goldsborough Apartments (formerly the Goldsborough Mort Wool Store).*

OTHER BRIDGES IN SYDNEY

Because early Sydney was built around the Harbour, bridges became an essential element in the pattern of development. Sydney has three major bridges – the Harbour Bridge (1932), the Gladesville Bridge (1964) and the Anzac Bridge (1996) – but there are many more. The commercial use of the Harbour determined the size and the shape of the bridges that crossed it: they either had to be high above the water, or had to open to allow ships to pass through.

Above: *The Opera House, with Farm Cove on the left, the CBD in the background, and Sydney Cove and Circular Quay on the right.*
Below: *(Left) View from Phillip Square on the west side of Sydney Cove and looking north towards the Harbour Bridge. (Right) Looking south towards Circular Quay.*

Above: *The City of Sydney towers in the background as a Manly ferry approaches Circular Quay with The Rocks on its right.*

CIRCULAR QUAY

The first European settlement in the Sydney area was established in 1788 on an inlet named Sydney Cove. The name given to the area by the local Aboriginal people was Warran or Werrong.

The Sydney Cove area developed as a port, and, in 1835, work began on the construction of a sea wall around the cove and the reclamation of the mudflats behind the wall at the southern end. By 1844, nearly four hectares of land had been reclaimed. The facility was horseshoe-shaped and was known as "Semi-Circular Quay". The "Semi-" was eventually dropped, and the area is now known as "Circular Quay".

Early in the twentieth century, the quay space on the southern side of Sydney Cove was converted to wharfage for ferry steamers. In the process, the arc of the original sea wall was gradually straightened so that it eventually enclosed a rectangular area.

Top: *(Left) The observation deck from Sydney Tower where a panoramic view of all of Sydney is possible. (Right) Sydney Tower looking towards the eastern suburbs and the Tasman Sea.* **Above:** *(Left) Sydney Tower and the monorail that runs in a clockwise loop from Darling Harbour to Chinatown to the CBD, and on to the western side of the city. (Right) Sydney Tower illuminated as dusk falls.*

SYDNEY TOWER

Sydney Tower (also known as AMP Tower) is situated over the Centrepoint Shopping Centre and, at 305 metres, is the tallest building in Australia. The tower has a shaft constructed of steel barrel-type units strengthened by external cables. On top of this is a four-storied turret connected to the ground by high-speed lifts and two stairways. There are revolving restaurants on levels 1 and 2 of the turret. On level 3 is a function room and coffee lounge, while level 4 is the observation deck. A spire bearing communication antennas extends 31 metres from the top of the turret.

Taronga Park Zoological Gardens was established at its present site in 1916. It was formerly on a site near the Sydney Cricket Ground that is now occupied by Sydney Girls' High School.

The steeply sloping site can be entered from the Harbour at the Taronga Wharf, where a chairlift or bus can transport visitors to the top. To view the exhibits, it is always better to start at the top and walk downhill.

The zoo has a wonderful collection of native and exotic animals. It also participates in an important conservation program to save endangered species from extinction.

Top: (Left) Looking from Taronga Zoo towards Cremorne Point, and the Bridge and city beyond. (Right) The giraffes at Taronga Zoo have an amazing view. **Above:** The Indian-inspired Elephant House with the city in the background.

Clockwise from top left: *Dixon Street, the focal point of Chinatown; the El Alamein Fountain at Kings Cross; the Cahill Expressway separating the Domain on the left from the Botanic Gardens on the right; looking towards the high altar of St Mary's Roman Catholic Cathedral; the columned entrance to the Art Gallery of New South Wales in the Domain; the George Street cinema area looking south towards Railway Square and Central Railway Station.*

Clockwise from top left: *The forecourt of the MLC Building near Martin Place; the Strand Arcade, which joins George Street with Pitt Street Mall; walking past a mural in Oxford Street, Paddington.*

OUT AND ABOUT IN SYDNEY

Different parts of Sydney offer different attractions. If you want fine Asian food and shopping, then Chinatown will be your venue. If you want bars and night life, try Kings Cross. If you want to see a film, it is likely to be showing in a cinema on George Street. If you want shopping, art galleries and good coffee, try Paddington. If the business world is your thing, the financial institutions from Martin Place to the Quay will satisfy your needs. If you want live performance, look for what's on at the Opera House or the Town Hall – and while you're near, drop in and sample the fabulous variety of food and splendid specialty shops in the Queen Victoria Building. If you wish to learn more about Australia, visit the Australian Museum or the Museum of Sydney. And if you want a quiet place in which to reflect, seek out the great cathedrals of St Andrew's near the Town Hall or St Mary's near the Australian Museum. Before entering St Mary's, have a look at the new spires that have capped the two towers of the south face.

Top: *(Left) The interior of the Queen Victoria Building showing the central clock, the galleries and the beautifully tiled floor. (Right) The clock tower of Sydney Town Hall.* **Bottom:** *The Queen Victoria Building looking down George Street towards the Quay.*

Above: *(Left) The Sydney Town Hall with its floodlit facade. (Right) The grand organ in the auditorium of Sydney Town Hall.*
Below: *(Left) The Australian Museum of Natural History. (Right) The fossilised skeleton of a dinosaur on display in the museum.*

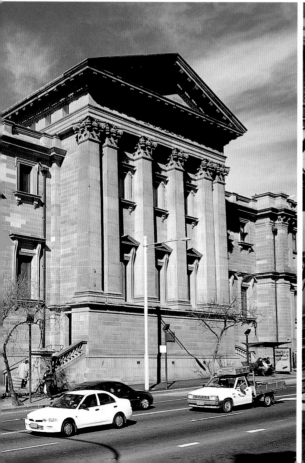

Clockwise from top left: *Governor Phillip Tower from the forecourt of the Museum of Sydney with the sculpture The Edge of the Trees in the foreground; sculptures in the Domain near the Art Gallery of NSW with Centrepoint in the background; statue of Apollo on the top of the Archibald Fountain in Hyde Park; the Anzac War Memorial in Hyde Park south; Governor Arthur Phillip statue and fountain in the Royal Botanic Gardens; duck ponds and ecological wetlands in the Royal Botanic Gardens.*

Clockwise from top left: *George Street North in The Rocks; the Lord Nelson Hotel, claimed to be the oldest licensed hotel in Australia; former bond stores bordering Campbells Cove, an inlet within Sydney Cove; Cadman's Cottage, Sydney's oldest house.*

Above: *Bondi Beach looking north.*
Below: *Bondi Beach looking out over the eastern suburbs with the high-rise buildings of the city in the background. The Bondi Pavilion is at the centre of the beach.*

BONDI AND THE SOUTHERN BEACHES

Bondi is one of the world's most famous beaches. Like all beaches in the Sydney region, Bondi is watched over by professional lifeguards and amateur lifesavers, who monitor an area of beach marked by flags. Bathing between the flags is compulsory and fines can be given for non-compliance.

During the 2000 Olympic Games, Bondi Beach was the venue for the beach volleyball, which was held in a special temporary stadium that could hold more than 10 000 spectators.

All the beaches in the eastern suburbs have their supporters. Each has something that makes it special. All are close to the mighty sandstone cliffs that define the coastline. All have marvellous rock platforms that support a rich and varied ecosystem. And all can be reached by public transport.

Clockwise from top left: *Maroubra Beach, the last major beach in Sydney's eastern suburbs; Bronte Beach is often troubled by strong rips; Coogee Beach on a warm weekend; Tamarama Beach is small, but has beautiful sand; an aerial of Coogee Beach.*

Above: *A sculpture by Helen Leete on the rock platform south of Manly Beach.*

MANLY AND THE NORTHERN BEACHES

The northern ocean beaches start at Manly and extend as far north as Palm Beach. Manly was named by Governor Arthur Phillip after the "manly bearing" of the Aboriginal people he met there on his first visit to the area in 1788. At Manly in 1902, newspaper editor William Gocher successfully challenged a law that banned recreational bathing during daylight hours.

Most of the northern beaches are very long; sometimes more than one surf lifesaving club serves one beach. For example, Manly Beach accommodates both Manly and Queenscliff Surf Lifesaving Clubs.

As you travel north up the coast, the sand becomes more coarse and the colour changes from pale yellow to a warmer reddish colour, stained by the iron compounds it contains.

Above: *Manly Beach is the ocean side of an isthmus that joins the Manly area to North Head. North Steyne and Queenscliff Beaches are at the northern end of Manly Beach.*
Below: *The Corso, the concourse joining Manly Beach to the Manly Ferry Wharf on Sydney Harbour.*

Above: *Barrenjoey Head and Lighthouse looking down on the surf of Palm Beach. The still waters of Barrenjoey Beach and Pittwater are on the right.*
Bottom: *(Left) Curl Curl Lagoon in the foreground and the channel to Curl Curl Beach, looking towards Manly Beach, North and South Heads and the entrance to Sydney Harbour. (Right) Avalon Beach looking west towards Clareville on Pittwater.*

Top: *Manly Beach with its distinctive Norfolk Island pines. The view is to the north towards North Steyne and Queenscliff Beaches.*
Middle: *A surf boat crashes through the breakers at the beginning of a surf boat race.*
Bottom: *Lifesavers competing in the march past at a surf carnival at Freshwater Beach.*

Above: *Stadium Australia, at the leading edge of sports stadium technology, site of the opening and closing ceremonies of the XXVII Olympiad.*

SPORTING SYDNEY

The high point of sport in Sydney was the staging of the XXVII Olympiad and the Paralympic Games in 2000. The focal point was the Homebush Bay area where swimming, athletics, archery, tennis, basketball, volleyball and football all were held. The Athletes' Village was located close by. Other Olympic venues included Darling Harbour, the Penrith rowing and whitewater courses, Horsley Park for equestrian events, Cecil Park for shooting, Blacktown for baseball and softball, Bankstown for cycling, and Bondi Beach for beach volleyball. All these facilities, with the exception of the beach volleyball stadium, have become permanent Sydney sporting venues.

However, there were many fine sporting facilities before the Olympics. Rugby League and Rugby Union have venues capable of seating thousands of fans and many of these, like the Parramatta Stadium, have been developed from local suburban ovals. One of the best loved cricket venues in the world is the Sydney Cricket Ground, which doubles as the home ground for the Sydney Swans, who play Australian Rules. As well as these, Sydney has four major thoroughbred racecourses, the most famous of which is Royal Randwick.

Above: *The Parramatta Football Stadium.* **Below:** *Stadium Australia, which holds upwards of 110 000 spectators, with the Superdome in the left background.*

Clockwise from top left: *A landscaped garden in autumn at Mount Wilson — the altitude makes spring and autumn particularly beautiful; Beauchamp Falls, one of the many spectacular falls in the Blue Mountains; the Three Sisters, pillars of eroded sandstone overlooking the Jamison Valley, are best seen from the lookout at Echo Point; the Scenic Railway is the world's steepest incline railway, and the bottom platform is connected to the Sceniscender by a 300-metre wooden boardwalk; the Sceniscender is a cable car at Scenic World that descends 545 metres onto the floor of the Jamison Valley.*

Above: *The Scenic Skyway is a horizontal cable car that takes passengers some 300 metres above the floor of the Jamison Valley to see spectacular views of the Three Sisters and the Katoomba Falls.*

THE BLUE MOUNTAINS

The Blue Mountains are on the World Heritage List. They are a hundred kilometres west of Sydney and have been a holiday playground for Sydney-dwellers since the 1880s. The mountains' name refers to the blue haze caused by droplets of eucalyptus oil exuded into the air by forests of gum trees.

The town of Katoomba is the focal point of the Blue Mountains. It has always been renowned for its guest houses, which are now supplemented by hotels and motels.

Sightseeing, bushwalking and golf are the main forms of recreation. There are several excellent restaurants and many art galleries that exhibit the work of local artists.

Beautiful gardens are a feature of many Blue Mountain towns such as Leura and Mount Wilson. The altitude brings forth exquisite blooms in spring and magnificent yellows and russet reds in autumn.

WOLLONGONG AND THE SOUTH COAST

Wollongong (the name is an Aboriginal word meaning "sound of the sea") is 80 kilometres south of Sydney. The largest city on the South Coast, it has its own university and technical college and a thriving commercial centre. Just south of Wollongong is Port Kembla, where the BHP Steelworks are located on an artificially created inner harbour. The area is backed by the Illawarra Escarpment where there are many coal mines.

The far south coast is now referred to as the Sapphire Coast. It is famous for its beautiful beaches, its fishing industry and its dairy industry.

Top left and clockwise: *The Fitzroy Falls, located west of Kiama in the Moreton National Park on the Illawarra Escarpment; the waters of the rich marine environment of Jervis Bay meet the Booderee National Park beach and dunes; Eastern Grey Kangaroos on the dunes of Murramarang National Park.*

Above: *(Left) Kiama Lighthouse, not far from the famous Kiama Blowhole. (Right) The broad sweep of the beach at Merimbula on the Sapphire Coast. in the far south of NSW.*
Below: *Wollongong is the only place on the east coast to have two lighthouses. The older (1871) marks the entrance to the Wollongong Harbour, created by building breakwaters out into the sea. The other (1936) is on Flagstaff Point, Wollongong Head.*

Above: *Looking south over the City of Gosford to Brisbane Water and the Brisbane Water National Park.*
Below: *(Left) The Entrance, where Tuggerah Lake enters the sea. (Right) Avoca Beach, Central Coast.*

Top: *A lone surf fisherman on Frazer Beach, Munmorah National Park.*
Bottom: *Terrigal Beach. Terrigal is a popular tourist destination and venue for conventions.*

THE CENTRAL COAST

The main settlement on the Central Coast is the city of Gosford. The towns in the Gosford area are either located on the coast or on the shores of Brisbane Water, which is the north-eastern arm of Broken Bay. Once a holiday resort for Sydney-dwellers, the Central Coast has become an area where residents daily commute to the city by electric train. Further north from Gosford is The Entrance, the town where Tuggerah Lake meets the sea. West of The Entrance and at the other side of Tuggerah Lake is the town of Wyong. The Entrance and Wyong are both popular tourist resorts.